Seven Places in America

To walker!
All best,

Seven

Places

in America

A Poetic Sojourn

by Miriam Sagan

Sherman Asher Publishing · Santa Fe

ISBN: 978-1-890932-42-8

Library of Congress Control Number: 2012915285

Book designed by Jim Mafchir
Cover image by Gail Reike

Sherman Asher Publishing
126 Candelario St.
Santa Fe, NM 87501
www.shermanasher.com

Manufactured in the U.S.A.

Acknowledgments

Greatest thanks are due to the programs and administrators that made these residences possible.

Some of these poems first appeared in *Santa Fe Poetry Broadside*, *South Florida Adventure*, *Harwood Center Anthology* "Looking Back To Place," 516 Arts "Book Lung: Poetry's Spin on Art," *The Moon*, *Origami Condom*, *New Mexico Poetry Review*, *Santa Fe Literary Review*, *Nuclear Free New Mexico Calendar*, *Adobe Walls*, and *Forest Reflections Log*.

Essays first appeared, in different forms, in *Haibun Today*, *Santa Fe Poetry Broadside*, and *Sage/Albuquerque Journal*.

Many thanks to Kathleen Lee, Carol Moldaw, and Richard Feidman for help with this manuscript.

Table of Contents

Introduction   *11*

American   14

I. Everglades
Introduction   **17**
Snail Villanelle   21
EVER/GLADE
   1. The Photograph   22
   2. Long Pine Key   24
   3. The Apartment   25
   4. Shark Valley   27
   5. The Folly   28
   6. Mirror   30
   7. 10,000 Islands   31
The Poinsetta   33
Native   34
Totem   35
The Visitor   36
Untitled 1   37
Sketches in a Notebook   38
Gulf Coast Solstice   40
The Slough   41

II. The Land/An Art Site
Introduction   *43*
Grass   46
LAUNDRY LINE KOAN
   0. The Approach   47
   1. Saint in a Landscape   49
   2. Two Blue Circles   51
   3. Nightsky   53
   4. An Open Field   55
   5. Salinas   57
   6. From Air to Air   58

III. Santa Fe River

Introduction   *59*

ON THE SANTA FE RIVER

    1. Randall Davey Audobon Center   62
    2. Cerro Gordo   63
    3. Alameda   65
    4. Alto Street   66
    5. Justice Department Santa Fe Internment Camp   68
    6. Frenchy's Field   69
    7. San Isidro Crossing   70

IV. Petrified Forest

Introduction   *71*

Rock Shop   74

VIEWS OF THE PAINTED DESERT

    1. The Tepees   75
    2. The Triassic   76
    3. Puerco Pueblo   78
    4. Painted Desert Inn   79
    5. Curio   80
    6. Dream   82

Recollection   83

Petrified Forest Haiku   84

Nizoni Point   86

From the Air Quality Monitoring Station   87

Black Field Sketch   89

V. Stone Quarry Hill

Introduction   *91*

Body Of   94

The Meditation Hut   95

Chittenango Falls   96

Into the Piney Woods   97

Tree House   98

Untitled #2   99

Oneida   100

Secret Garden Trail   102

Seneca Falls   103

Stone Quarry Hill   105

Erie Canal   106

VI. Mounds

Introduction   *109*
Mound   112
Midden   114
Serpent Mound   115
vessel, urn, skull   117
Newark Earthworks   118
Hunter   120
Untitled #3   121

VII. Andrews Experimental Forest

Introduction   *123*
Mushroom Pantoum   126
An Autobiography in Trees   127
Rustic   128
Reflection Points   129
A Different Forest   131
Two Tanka   132
Forest Haiku   133
Aubade   134
What Am I?   135
Untitled #4   136
Spore Point   137
Nocturne   138

Notes   *141*

Introduction

"Place is a special kind of object—an object in which one can dwell." Yi-Fu Tuan in *Space and Place: The Perspective of Experience.*

Over a three year period, I left home numerous times to go some place unfamiliar. Some journeys took me more than a thousand miles, some just a few hours. But all were forays into the unknown. As a writer, I was looking for the freshness of seeing things in a new way. As a middle-aged woman, I was looking for a sense of self outside of my roles as mother, wife, daughter, and teacher. At times I didn't know what I was looking for, and at times I was a pilgrim on a quest. On all my journeys I was looking for borderlines, most particularly the border that earthwork artist Robert Smithson called the "slurb"—the border between the suburban and the wild.

I grew up in northern New Jersey. (Interestingly, so did Smithson). As a child, I lay in bed late at night reading about the archeology of Troy, the Maya's sacrificial well. Surely something lay beneath my suburban existence. I just couldn't find it. Digging a garden, we turned up a broken Dutch tile, edged in pale green. I was as excited as if we'd found a Viking burial. Throughout my life, and in many ways, I continued to look for what was buried.

Seven Places in America really began with my relationship to the National Parks. When I was almost twelve, my family took a vacation by train to the Grand Canyon. What I saw completely changed my New Jersey eyes. For many years I visited the parks, and wrote in them. This process became formal with a residency at Everglades National Park and continued with the Petrified Forest. The Everglades was itself a series of boundary lines. My private theme for being there was how one kind of space turned to another, water to land, agriculture to everglade. National Parks tell the visitor where—and how—to look. They direct our attention to marvels, but my process was also to look in nooks and crannies, off the beaten path, at destruction as well as beauty. In the Petrified Forest time was a concrete thing. Erosion showed geologic time as clearly as a wall calendar. But space and time do meet. The geographer Yi-Fu Tuan notes that space has a temporal meaning and that time is also a measure of distance. In this intersection, I wrote my poems.

Two of the places were art sites—The Land in Mountainair, New Mexico and Stone Quarry Hill Art Park in Cazenovia, New York. Both pieces of land were beautiful but essentially ordinary—except for the fact that so much attention had been paid to their topography and meaning by so many artists. Both places felt saturated by vision. The land had been marked, changed, and interpreted, by other people. Working on these sites was like walking into a collective dream. Robert Smithson said "the physical site is a destination...a 'tour'; recalled through snapshots and travelogues." By definition I was a tourist in these new places where my residence was brief and temporary. And my souvenirs were words.

My project had two sites that I thought of as lines—and interestingly both involved rivers. One was the Santa Fe River, just a few blocks from my house, and one was the line of archeological sites of the civilizations that built the mounds along the Ohio and Mississippi. These were the more personal sites for me—I had determined them and although both sparked plenty of interest I wasn't a designated writer-in-residence at either. Both close to home and far away, these were more places to wander through than to live.

The last place of the project was the Andrews Experimental Forest in Oregon. By seeming coincidence, it combined many aspects of the other places. It was a designated place with a purpose, like the national parks. It even had three reflection spots for each writer-in-residence to write about. These long term ecological reflection spots, like the art sites, were repositories of multiple visions. And like the rivers, Andrews was a place about watersheds, a small place in the larger context of ecosystem. I went to Andrews innocently. Unlike my other forays I had little idea or theme when I went. I had done no reading, or research. It was late autumn, cool, rainy, dark. If the forest had an unconscious mind, I had fallen into it, or perhaps into my own. When I woke up I realized that I had been working on a book all along. And that I had only understood this once the book was done.

"Solitude is a condition for acquiring a sense of immensity" writes Yi-Fu Tuan. My longest residency was two weeks, not a long time by the standards of Thoreau's cabin at Walden Pond, or by May Sarton's *Journal of A Solitude*. However, In my own life, two weeks felt substantial and lavish.

Alone, I was bolder and also more self-indulgent than within my family. I could drive long distances by myself, and also eat something odd for supper at 4 pm. It was a delightful benefit to become reacquainted with a kind of essential self. This self was at home in unfamiliar surroundings, developing in quiet and darkness.

It wasn't always easy to explain what I was doing. Some of my friends loved to hike and camp in nature, but I wasn't doing that. Writers I knew enjoyed the leisure and pleasant surroundings of an artist's colony, but this was different than that as well. People would ask me if I was frightened—presumably of something like an alligator or the company of my own mind. Implied too in the questions was the implication that the questioner would be bored to death doing this. But that was what I sought—a simple, even funky, habitation where I could be alone.

"Where is the nearest jelly doughnut?" my father wanted to know when I called him from the Everglades. I found this amusing, because not everyone considers the doughnut to be an indicator of civilization. But my father and I are both fond of them. The nearest jelly doughnut might be in a box in my temporary kitchen, at the end of Flamingo, in Gallup or Holbrook, at a country store or a local farmers' market, at a fast food place in exurbia or the Dunkin Doughnuts a few blocks from my usual house.

It is not possible to shed the old self just by changing geography. But it is possible to expand that self so it includes not just a jelly doughnut but a more permeable boundary between self and landscape—the terrain of a poem.

American

Tim Prythero
mixed media, 1988

The trailer is pale blue and white
With pink striped awnings, a pink flamingo
On the door. Saguaro cactus with an owl in the yard
And a Madonna in a blue stucco shell
Or an inverted bathtub.
A kitschy statue of a boy in a sombrero
Pulls a burro...this is the border
But between what and where?
I admire the "American" trailer as always
Next to the Women's Room at the Albuquerque airport
My usual point of departure
This time for Fort Lauderdale, where I'll sleep
At a Ramada lit by tiki torches
Fake Polynesian effect around the pool
Where plastic flowers entwine
With real multivariegated leaves
And dreams border on the subtropics.

I had house guests, once,
Who wanted to see "the real" city of Santa Fe
Which they'd heard had gotten fake
By real, they meant the old fake, not the new—
Fred Harvey thunderbird designs in silver
Or rugs woven, pots painted, for the tourist trade
But old enough so the motive fades
And makes an image of the authentic.
They didn't mean they wanted to see the "real real" city
Of gang graffiti, drunk drivers, or my usual trips
To the orthodontist or Ross Dress for Less.
And at Jackalope—Folk Art by the Truckload—
They were confused

14

By my enthusiasm
Pulling out of a cluttered bin
A necklace of tiny plastic birds and animals
With a "carved" turquoise plastic bear
And my delight—look!
Fake Zuni jewelry!

I bought the fake and hung it on my neck
I'd always wanted a fake fetish necklace
Made in Asia.
I was at Zuni once
Before Easter, in the rain
The hornos were steaming in the plaza
Smoke filled the air
Streets ran mud, and I did buy

Inlaid turquoise and silver, a dragonfly
Concrete and yet approximate
Like any souvenir.

I

Everglades National Park, Florida, December 2006: An Exotic Solitude

It took me a day and a half to get from Santa Fe in northern New Mexico to the Everglades in southern Florida. I left a busy life of family and teaching for more than two weeks of almost uninterrupted solitude. As I pulled up to the Park Service offices I had a moment of terror—what if I'd made the whole thing up and the residency wasn't real? I was reassured to meet Alan Scott, the ranger in charge of the artists in residence program. He gave me a brief orientation to the park, which focused on:

The Four Poisonous Snakes Of The Park
The Two Poisonous Plants
Mosquitoes, And West Nile Virus
Why To Never Touch A Caterpillar
When To Back Away From An Alligator (if it hisses and comes toward you)

Then he took me outside to a convienantly located poison wood tree covered in poison ivy vines and had me identify each one.

"Now," said Alan "on to the dangers of man." Serial killers? Psychopaths? "People drive worse on vacation than they do at home," he said "be careful, particularly in parking lots."

The apartment I was to stay in looked simple but pleasant, despite its scuffed linoleum and obvious years of wear, and turned out to be a great place to write. The first thing I did was move my desk—card table really—to the screened porch, facing into the forest of slash pine. I decided to limit my housekeeping to boiling some mildewed sponges and arranging things in a mild way. I didn't want to replicate domestic life. I was here to write and explore. I investigated the three sections of the park, and surrounding areas. I went in search of the rare and unusual—and was rewarded by seeing crocodiles who favor the brackish waters of the bay and a nest of a baby alligators. It turns out these toothy reptiles are devoted mothers, who tend their offspring for a full two years. I saw anhingas, turquoise-eyed cormorants, egret, ibis, cranes...a panoply of birds to observe and admire. But what I was most in search of was the rare tree snail. After several hours in a tropical hammock, a hardwood island in the usual sea of grass, I found one shining exquisitely in the gloom. Later, on a ranger's tip, I saw a cluster of multicolored shells in a slash pine forest.

One day I counted almost a hundred turkey vultures riding the thermals above my house. I was just a few minutes from the Royal Palm Visitor Center and the Anhinga Trail. A few years ago, I'd made a dash of a day trip through here and part of my motivation was to come back—and simply sit and look. I walked the boardwalk around the slough almost every day. Each time I saw something new. I saw a cormorant catch a catfish—it is the only bird that has figured out how to eat catfish—bludgeon it and break its spine and swallow it in one gulp.

I wanted to make a poetic map of the park. The poem was getting bigger and bigger, then finally settled into seven sections. Some sections required actually going somewhere—some moved in time and imagination. I went to Flamingo, and out among the mangroves, to Shark Valley and to the Gulf Coast and by boat among 10,000 Islands. And there were things I didn't see—a panther, not even a bobcat. No pythons, either, those unwelcome visitors. I also explored the border of the park, agricultural lands that interrupt the water flow, the Redland area and Krome Avenue, nurseries I would have simply thought lush and charming if I hadn't been focused on water drainage and wilderness preservation.

There was a journal that each artist had written in. Alan Scott had suggested I not read it right away, and that was a good idea—I had my own experience first. It surprised me, though, when I did read it, how similar everyone's experience was—the bliss of being in such beautiful surroundings combined with intense inspiration to create. The only conflict described, one which I shared, was whether to work or to jaunt about. One artist had drawn a detailed image of a green leaf and one of a snail.

I felt a familiar twinge of jealousy—of the ability to reproduce the world visually. Still, I found that here I was working as a poet almost the way painters must work—going out, looking at something, recording it in my notebook.

The artist who was in the apartment before me had left me a big board covered in foil. The first thing I did was put up a map of the Everglades. Then came photographs by my friend Mary Peck that had been exhibited at Miami-Dade Community College. The images of the park were in black and white, meditative long horizontals. Then I added three postcards of birds, including one ibis and one egret. I had trouble telling them apart and was plagued by not knowing which bird I'd actually seen. I kept changing them in a poem, changing the sound, trying to get it right. I hung up a pair of beautiful, long, beaded earrings and an even more lavish turquoise, white, yellow, red and black necklace. Women at the Miccosukee Indian cultural center had helped me match them. Over it all, I pinned up a painting of a model of the solar system. Why? I guess because I felt far from home but also at home in a vast space.

On the boat out of 10,000 Islands I met a family from Pasadena. The woman and I got to chatting, and at the end she exclaimed : "I've never met an author before!" I, on the other hand, had never seen white pelicans before—hundreds of them taking off from a sandbar.

Natural beauty I had expected, but I was a little nervous about solitude. My day concluded with a few errands, coming home, maybe more writing, an early idiosyncratic supper of whatever I wanted—like an avocado with seaweed salad—and early tropic sunset. There was no radio, television, or VCR in the apartment. I did have a phone, though, and intermittent access on a laptop so I could usually check my e-mail. I lay on the couch, reading a book, listening to palm fronds in the wind.

Solitude is not loneliness. Loneliness is a sense of disconnection. The reason it is easy to feel lonely in a crowd is that there is no intimacy. The same is true of loneliness within a deteriorating relationship or unhappy situation. The mere physical presence of others doesn't guard against loneliness, indeed can even exacerbate it. Solitude is the state of physical aloneness, but often coupled with a sense of greater connection—even simply to a sense of self.

My daughter Isabel, then seventeen, called me twice during that retreat—once to say her cell phone had been stolen, once to say she'd gotten into the college of her choice. Each time, her voice yanked me from the free-floating state of aloneness to the highly focused maternal state. I was looking for that self who isn't just a set of roles—mother, wife, daughter, and sister. That self can get lost in the daily shuffle. But she reemerged with time and space.

Sometimes I did get lonely, Then I might write a friend, or call home. Or I might go out and walk among palm trees and a fresh-water slough teeming with birds, fish, alligators, and turtles. One afternoon, I watched a man trap a butterfly and put it in his car. Another woman, who turned out to be a European tourist, and I glared at him—his act was both illegal and unpleasant. Sensing rather than seeing us, he opened the door and let the butterfly fly free. She and I smiled, and struck up a momentary complicit acquaintance.

Snail Villanelle

On the Gumbo Limbo Trail—
Shining white luminescence—
I finally saw the tree snail.

Color of mother-of-pearl,
Rare as a Transit of Venus,
On the Gumbo Limbo Trail.

Whorled, slow-moving shell
Out of Cuba, the liguus
I finally saw the tree snail.

These patterns inspire calico shawls,
Rickrack and zig-zag and fuss,
On the Gumbo Limbo Trail.

One moon in the sky, pale spiral—
Simply its nature to please us—
I finally saw the tree snail.

Far-off, one white sail
As on the sea, the phosphorescence.
On the Gumbo Limbo trail
I finally saw the tree snail.

EVER/GLADE

1. The Photograph

edge, cloud, horizon
swoop
    of winged scavengers
buzzards over the sea of grass
far-lying hammock of trees
distant as the past
or the photograph you once took
of the tiny columned temple
classical, size of a thumbprint
in the corner

some views by nature
are panoramic
this watercourse
with Egyptian walking ibis in profile
and anhingas, wings stretched,
crucified like saints,
hung our to dry

you took a photograph of me
once, as well
pregnant, in a fedora hat
clinging to my then husband...
wind, gray sky, vulture tipped wing
shapes repeat themselves
and words must also, bromeliad,
eat the air
horizon line is everything here
it is the only thing

blue hammock, mahogany hammock
an inverse island against fire,

tropics sunk in limestone:
liana, vine, the strangling fig
where poisonwood
becomes a tree
that eats itself
(avoid it in the rain)
black speckled leaves and black sap
corrode
but also have some meaning in the scheme

drop tip
of leaf shape
channels rain,
you don't want to be the same
want to cross
from one place to the next
as god must divide
water from dry land
   again and again
what did you long to see
at long last on the bay
by the marina's sway—
one more point of departure
open water
pelican sandbar
and in the magnified view—imagined Cuba or fabled
Indies...

2. Long Pine Key

I don't see it
and the panther
does not see me—
beast who steps
quieter than nightfall

gangly pines wait
for fire
to germinate—
palm fronds' noisy rattle,
I wait for the panther

orange butterfly
white star orchid-shaped
orchid
no panther
slash pines in wind

3. The Apartment

My grandmother used to say
When someone or other died
That they had "gone to Florida."
We believed her, and years later might inquire
After the So-and-sos and their bridge game
Only to discover they were long gone.

In the dark New York apartment
When I was three, my father coughed
Till he was sent to cure bronchitis
To Palm Beach, and sent me
Two postcards which in mind's eye I can see
One—pink flamingos, the other—
Characteristic clustered shape of pelicans.

Today, I try to understand the world
From this screened porch—
Landscape that lies low as my childhood,
The Cape, the Jersey Meadowlands,
And holds the same three colors:
    sand
    sky
     scrub green
Here, clouds pass above slash pines
Ants dig pits by the front steps
And I don't dream of other places.

Whoever lived here before me
Left behind
Five I-Ching coins, silver set in gold,
But no Book of Changes.
And an indigo kimono hung on a nail

Surely by mistake
I'm tempted to try it on
But don't, a superstition
From a fairy tale as if a poisoned dress,
Invisibility cloak.

I want to stay visible to myself.
It's dangerous to sleep
Night after night
In a bed slept in by strangers.
I opened every door
Aired out the stale smell of dreams.
A button the floor,
A mop, a broom, a rancid sponge,
Pine cones dropped on the doorstep
As if by UPS, or the wind,
And a string of colored Xmas lights,
Something at dusk
To decorate
A solitude.

4. Shark Valley

I'll take no photograph
of what I can remember
low-lying sedge, bayhead island
    dahoor holly
    wax myrtle
    coco plum
    willow
and the gumbo limbo
whose name
sounds like a carousel
whose wood
was used to carve
merry-go-rounds
these trees usually found
below the Tropic of Cancer

a nest of baby
alligators
a dozen or more
surprisingly touching
not yet the toothy beasts
they'll become
but watched over for years
by their mother hidden in amphibious shadow
where water meets air

past fifty myself
I'm still trying
to perfect the mix
of getting somewhere
and being there...

5. The Folly

Bougainvillea, acres of it
Induced rainbow
In the irrigation arc
Spray of water, stink
Of nitrogen.
The land is flat, enriched, it yields
Huge alligator pears, and
Who doesn't like an orange.
The flag of Cuba waves
Over the nursery, the colors of Mexico,
Potted poinsettias.
It's paradise, the only trouble is
The flower is the serpent here,
This plowing of the soil
As old as Ur
Destroys the wild.

At the car rental
The man speaking Farsi
Checks in the woman
Who says in her accent
She has not spoken Latvian
In twenty-five years.
The turnpike rolls through tollbooths
Till it ends
At giant Walmart.
And from there
Continue on past Circle K
Past Robert's fruit stand
Where they also sell
Boxes embossed with tiny shells
And cowries carved

To each sign of the zodiac.
And then go on
Downstream by inches,
This sea of sedge
Is massive river slow,
To Flamingo Bay
Where there have never been
Flamingos.

A man builds a castle of coral
Curved and crested like topiary
An oddity, a vision, like Miami
That rises to the Atlantic side.
Globe warms,
Coral dies
And the sea
Will rise.
Meanwhile, without rest, the pickers
Squat and harvest
In the rows,
Beneath straw hats, in worn, bleached clothes
They make a sad calico
Quilted from their need and other's greed
Across the field.
Pastel, the edge of rundown town
In the rain
Buildings painted pink, lavender, pale green
By the prison's razor wire
And the truck with melons.
And along the side of the road
The poor go on walking
As they do
Everywhere.

6. Mirror

navigating by the black mirror

faint stars of the sixth magnitude

cormorant's eye turns turquoise

motel shuttered by hurricane

meridian

on the card table, *The Collected Wallace Stevens*

a nonrepresentational painter and a horizon line

fluorescent resin

the glass-bottomed boat, electric blue aquarium in the bar, the
transparent woman
   at the museum of science

homing instinct, a magnetic chip in the brain

the sea was not a mirror

emptiness...

silver palm reflected in the dark pool

7. 10,000 Islands

Mangrove roots
Coated in oyster shells—
This is a border
As surely as between Ciudad Juarez and El Paso del Norte
Between sleep and waking
Between the evening star and his wife the morning star
Between the living and the dead
This is the border
Between land and water
That first division
After darkness and light

The mind may be persistent
Even more so the mangrove roots
Red, black, white
A mangle
Where pods propagate by floating
Into the tea dark water
The anaerobic soil, the marl
Breathing tubes in the brackish bay

Shell islands
Left by those long gone—
You'll try and see the pattern,
Let the eye
Arrange a meaning
10,000 islands printed on the day
Like 10,000 cranes on kimono fabric

I longed for departure
As if it were love
As if it would take me out

Of myself, of my accustomed way—
Sandbar of white pelicans
Lifts off, wheels into the sun
Silver flash of fish before the prow
Maze of low islands, one after the other,
Gives way
To open water.

The Poinsettia

I bought a potted poinsettia—
Dark pink, pale red—
As if I were a painter

And set it on my table
To describe. It's not
What you see at first, look closely to be able

To discern green foliage called bracts
Blush carmine or flamingo beneath
Tiny yellow true flowers.

It sat there as the hours
Passed, and days, as I ate
My quiet meals

And drank my lonely sugared tea.
Beauty surrounded me like grace
And when the time came

For me to leave this place
I missed the red of Aztec flower,
Bold solitude's face.

Native

the python
does not belong
here,
not just the proverbial snake
in Eden
but invasive
liberated from a pet store
glass aquarium
to stalk the glade

tilapia, too,
eventually too big
for stork to eat
competes for nests
with the local fish

bear, turtle, panther
and humankind
molded from mud
into the Fourth World
climb from the pit into air

I also come from elsewhere

Totem

Strangler fig has a firm grasp
On the palmetto, like some
Very slow-moving python.
Outside the park ranger's house
A giant plastic inflatable snow globe
Presents Santa and Frosty beneath an endless blizzard.
"Let It Snow!" the globe proclaims
On humid mornings, rainy afternoons
In the Everglades.

Outside the Miccosukee Indian restaurant
Are two odd totem poles, black, yellow, red
Looking like Pacific Northwest thunderbirds
With a lot of teeth
Or alligators with stiff wings.
Inside, the usual, fry bread, tribal cops, unsweetened ice tea
And the lady waiting for takeout
Her t-shirt emblazoned PUBLIC ENEMY.

I also put things together
That don't belong together:
Vitamins, and the tree snail shell
From Thailand,
The doll in necklace and bead earrings
Purple rickrack on her yellow dress,
The potted poinsettia, the menorah
Of tea lights arranged on an upsidedown
Baking pan.
And the photographs
Of what is beyond my screened porch—
Tangled lianas, bay islands
All untitled, simply toned silver print
As if it were best   ·
To simply look.

The Visitor

buzzards ride the thermals
over the slash pine forest

I don't know the neighbors
but their dreams seep through the cinder block wall

a smell comes from the sea
or of a solitary supper, cooked early

the little house with its metal awning
the neglected purple ice plants by the screen door

the day is not a mask I put on
and the bay is not a mirror

if I didn't know better
I'd say I was all alone

writing on lined paper
trying to perfect just one line

even in my sleep
the argument with the dead goes on

two saw palmettos—I think of them as mine—
rattle day and night in the wind

as noisy as the unexpected visitor
who arrives in minutes, or years

the one who keeps me waiting
the one who never appears.

Untitled #1

The yellow bench
in the sad garden
of spices

I see you pause
reading the book
marking the page with your finger

you've been dead
a long time
almost a dozen years

but here in the subtropics
you appear, as if in life
reading a book about birds

and smile the smile
that was yours alone to smile
ironic, a little wistful

as if surprised
by Fortune

yellow fruit has fallen to the ground
I was not here
to hear it make a sound of something overripe

and when I listen
for the rustle of the pages
of the turning book

you've gone away again
as I always
knew you would

Sketches in a Notebook

a lizard
living
in a rolled up shade

tree bromeliads—
two cormorants
build a nest of twigs

man with a cane
crosses paths with
a tiny turtle

child pats the palm tree
ignores
the alligator

tree canopy
butterfly, and purple glade
morning glory

rare buttonwood vine
looks like any foliage—
but rare...

a leaf drops in
the mahogany hammock—
without season

out of the palm trees
a peacock darts—escaped—
but from where?

tree snail gleams
in the leaf canopy—
stolen ghost orchid

raindrops' circles—
yellow spatterdock flowers
floating green pads...

two shy vultures
pick raindrops
off the car's roof

only the most
delicate colored pencils
draw the tree snail's shell

cypresses
drawn in an inky line,
overcast afternoon

leaf's
drop tip
implies rain

Gulf Coast Solstice

dwarf pond cypresses
standing ghostly in winter
give way

to a beach town
like any other
on the verge of rain

trying to make sense of the past
or to meditate
purely on the palm

the houses in a row
are pink, blue, green
or—pink with a green roof
    aqua
    lime

gray clouded sunset
2 boys + a girl
in a low quarrel by the verandah

a yellow house
with green shutters
on stilts

if this is beauty—don't
hold back
if this is suffering—the same

light leaves the town towards the bay
estuary,
the shaggy palms, no moon

The Slough

I left the slough and solitude
The moon tipped over like a cup

I left blue heron, green heron
Crane, egret, ibis

The crowd of fish in a sea of sedge
That draws alligator, wading bird

I did not take
The glass-bottomed boat to the stormy reef

What I saw
I saw also in the mind's eye

Requiring not just beauty
But belief

Tangerines piled high
In the dark glazed bowl

I went out begging
In nights saturated with dream

Between sleep and waking
Storm's whiteout

So many icicles dripping
One moon

II

The Land/An Art Site, August 2007-August 2008: The Familiar Made Strange

The Land/An Art Site is forty acres of land, pinon and juniper, in Mountainair, New Mexico. It is a kind of artistic incubator. Tom Cates and E. Nuevo are the artists who founded and curate it. In some ways, it is land like any other acreage in New Mexico. Yet in some ways it is magically apart.

I wrote to The Land with a loose proposal—I wanted to write a poetic map of the place. The response was unequivocal—I was welcome to a residency, but it was I as an artist who was being accepted, not my specific proposal. I was told The Land itself had a way of transforming vision.

"What are you doing?" my husband Rich wanted to know. I was worrying, lying on the living room couch and staring into space. "I'm installing a poem I haven't written on a site I've never seen," I said. I was so worried I went to a Sam Peckinpah movie that was showing at SITE Santa Fe before lunch. I ran into educator Juliette Myers there. I told her I was worried the land was blank. "Nothing is blank, darling," she counseled me. That became the first line of my poem.

Rich and I went down in the heat of an August day and met Tom and Edite. A chain gate opened, a rutted road led to the site. A few things were permanent—Steve Peters' little benches carved with text that recorded sounds over the twenty four hours of a day. Most installations were low-impact or no-impact. A beautifully shaped arroyo curved away. A train whistled. I was hooked. On our way home we stopped in Albuquerque to go shoe shopping. I couldn't function in the strip mall. I was totally overwhelmed. All those signs and letters seemed like messages—marks on the landscape. My point of view had changed.

I went to Mountainair that autumn and stayed in the Shaffer

Hotel. The Shaffer became part of my experience. A historic hotel, its ceiling was painted wildly by a former owner. A devil's head smirked from a mosaic wall. It was purported to be haunted. I wrote in a small dark room, on a little desk. For two nights, I was the only guest, making forays out to The Land, which looked increasingly luminous. The pueblo of Abo, conquered by the Spanish, stood nearby, ruined yet splendid. Later stays at the Shaffer would find me in larger, airier rooms, and once even all by myself in the honeymoon suite. But that first room was the womb-like space that generated much of the structure of the work.

I saw The Land under snow that winter with my friend Hope Atterbury. She took some photographs that helped focus the images in my mind. I began to write my poem. In the section "Saint in a Landscape" I used a quote from the patron saint of the project, Robert Smithson, who said "earth's surface and the figments of the mind have a way of disintegrating." It was both an explanation and a handy excuse for my confusion as I moved into the unknown. Rich and I went back in the spring to watch the sun go down and the stars come out on a moonless night. My sense of topography of the place had begun to include the sky above. A visit to the nearby salt lakes, and a museum show of the artist Basia Irland, came in as influences on the section "Salinas."

When the poetic map was written, something changed. The challenge had always been to get the words into the landscape in some temporary manner. I began to see those words fluttering in the breeze, disintegrating like a line of Tibetan prayer flags. But how? I've always had a love of laundry lines—and laundry itself. My backyard housed an old line, and a heap of decrepit wooden pins. How about a laundry line on The Land? I asked Dan Stubbs, a fine woodworker, and partner of my friend Ana Matiella. Could he build me a line?

It would be ranch style, old fashioned, he proclaimed. He scavenged the wood from an old corral, surprising the owner by offering to buy it. The lines would be wire. I needed to weather some pins. I bought some and put them out in a little basket to deteriorate. "I brought your clothespins in," Rich said, in a big rainstorm. Back out they went. The text, though, presented a problem. It obviously could not be the whole poem. I started fooling around, taking one line from each section, and adding one more to represent the Shaffer Hotel.

But when I recited the selection at the opening of The Land's gallery in Albuquerque it fell flat. "Hang on," I told the audience. "I think this is in the wrong order." So I read it backwards, half-terrified to be working spontaneously in public, and luckily it sounded right:

nothing is secret

haunted corridors, a ghost in every mirror,

braille of the book of salt

the spirit boat, the chain linked fence

stars come out in nightsky, cryptobiotic

did this create

tiny scenes of the narrative,

this is where I began building a scale model of solitude

This then became the text to install. I had it printed—vinyl letters on a tablecloth. Allegra Print cautioned me that eventually the letters would fall off, but that felt just right. A year after I had first visited The Land, Dan installed the laundry line. Ana added some embroidered material and fabric scraps. The text was officially hung a few weeks later as part of the Sunflower Poetry Festival in Mountainair. I added a gauze dress and the slip of my wedding dress to balance the look of the laundry line. And left the basket of clothespins beneath it.

I hear that pack rats stole them.

Grass

the only thing
this web catches
is dew

bell bowl
sounds in meditation—
who dropped
a smooth stone
into still water

weaving the grasses
into a nest—
just the wind

spider webs
at every fence post
on barbed wire—
those white grasses
nameless as smoke

your hair turns white
photographing
this world of grass

kiva shape
sunk in the earth, Abo's
mission church—
hawk's red underwing
blush of conquered stones

what rustles
these dry grasses—
the golden wind

LAUNDRY LINE KOAN

0. The Approach

Nothing is blank, darling.
A space defined
Is something.

map on the dashboard
reflected in the windshield

open field
telephone poles
morning, word, memory

the actual map
the actual road

the little towns
that lost their post offices

tequila bottles
shining like planets
at the edge of the road

the decayed hotel
chandelier
of melting candles
   or icicles
circle of wax
water

the train
that comes through every seven minutes
the museum
of my childhood

the museum
of my adolescence

white   door   crumpled paper
curtain
piano keys
motion
    in this otherwise

the train that comes through
every seven years

a room full of sand
how I couldn't cross
the open basin
had to walk the straight line
along the tracks

lines
might outline shapes
move independently of color fields
exist behind or within

the train comes through
every seven seconds

boxcars
sky
this is where I begin buiding
a scale model
of solitude

fall asleep
on the topo map
spread on the bed
and ask:
who am I?

1. Saint in a Landscape

cliff crag, castle, cave—
in the background of the painting
tiny scenes of the narrative
nativity, the worship of beasts
not exactly
the past, or what led to this
but as in memory
a panoramic scene
of simultaneity
the journey, the rest, the destination
and in the foreground
the little saint
contemplates the skull's jaw
and the lion
tamed by pain
extends his injured paw

of course I remember you as a baby
but it's not the same "you"
caterpillar and butterfly
don't compose an "I"
nor does cocoon

frescoes of trees
inside the house
outside, a maze of boxwood
might signify
the world, its twists and turns.
a book of dirt, paper, branches
a nest, a spirit house,
a winter dwelling.
"earth's surface

and the figments of the mind
have a way of disintegrating."
archeology of the pack rat's midden
who knows, you tell yourself,
these seeds of ancient grasses
might sprout again.

2. Two Blue Circles

The artist
Wanted to plant
A circle of bluebonnets here
But they wouldn't grow
In the desert soil.
Instead, he constructed
A circle of blue glass.

The neighbors were meth addicts
Hard characters, who yelled
And fought. When the screaming started
Their children went into
The circle of blue glass—
Stood in the center
Of a safe place.

Another artist
Also wanted to build a circle
On the land.
He sent exact
Specifications by mail
Dimensions to be raked
Into the earth.
But this did not create
A perfect circle in sod.
Rather, it eroded, and a gopher
Dug a hole in the perimeter.
Then it rained
And the circle's interior
Bloomed with flax.
The circle was filled with blue flowers.

A third circle,
Drawn in blue chalk
On the sidewalk
By me as a girl
Washes away in the rain.

3. Nightsky

Antelope, jack rabbits, dusk
Comes on
Civil twilight, then nautical
As if light were a little ship
Slipping over the horizon
    Sirius, Dog Star brightest
    at this latitude
Contrails like speedboat wake
Give way to velveteen sky
Saturn, whose rings we can't see
Without the binoculars
We left on the shelf at home,
Castor and Pollux
Shining on either side.
And gradually, like invisible ink
The constellations you point out
Begin to define themselves
Dipper, Orion, the city of Albuquerque faint glow to the north.
Stars come out in nightsky, cryptobiotic
Mark direction
As clearly as in the planetarium.
Planes above us headed somewhere else
I'd like to know
Where
And how each passenger
Is doing, reading, dozing,
Worrying about the past
As ice clinks in plastic cups.
Try painting all this
With whiteout
On carbon paper.
On earth

The flying star weed called
Datura.
I'm cold, now, ready
To go
You say—"you do the Cliff Notes
Of altered states."
Aldebaran, Betelgeuse, Procyon
And smoke from the Manzanos
Burning all night
Highway flashing sign
FIRE ACTIVITY AHEAD.
These stars
Like the ceiling
Of the Shaffer Hotel:
Lion's head, masked dancers, backwards swastikas of migration
Thunderbird, lightning zigzag, a narrative of relocation.
These stars
By dawn
Will unfold their wings
And fly away again
Like mourning doves in the yard below us.

4. An Open Field

the boat of the mind
    that floats on air

mobile of empty bottles
    clustered like honeycomb
    wasp's nest cell

a retaining wall in the arroyo
or something revealed

coracles of dream
    so far from water

a nest of air
    the spirit boat

the photographer vanishes
    into the act of seeing

we disappear
    off our own shadows

birdless   a little wind

beauty's paranoia
these arrangements of meaning

bluebirds! a half dozen
western russet breasts

a post in the middle
I won't say—nowhere

white/grasses
    plucked like broken harp strings
    the abandoned zither

of wind
wind's chasm

a sound—metallic—without a source
but the other world

the chain link fence
we left carelessly draped
is tightly closed

and when we leave
a flicker's feather
comes to hand

5. Salinas

blind, you'll taste
the braille
of the book of salt
of wave's slap
or blood
on the lip

great salt flats
    cracked
like glaze (like hieroglyph)

pockets full
    of black stones
    the soil of your
    native land
tossed over the shoulder
    to keep off
        the evil eye
like bread

pink salt core
raised bumps
where is it
safe
to touch?

dissolving letters
in the museum of water

6. From Air to Air

geography, which speaks of war,
the presence or absence of salt,
landscape as koan, the visible world—
even at the edge of sleep I see it
Abo ruins, a raven, masonry frames only turquoise sky,
decaying arc of tied branches in the stone arroyo
to say: these are our mountains
is to say
something specific, intentional, controvertible

follow a line, a path, a zigzag, of fabric and scraps,
Kandinsky ribbon laid like aboriginal songline,
but instead of a great rock as container
of the world it is the dream that perplexes—
furniture draped in dustsheets,
wallpaper, a slide of stained cells, buttons,
a petaled circle—
pasting beads and yarn to paper
the artist—or child—
concentrates
outside, a crow lights on a fence post
or yellow buses creak down Broadway
nothing is secret.

III

Santa Fe River, Summer, 2007: Water Fills My Dreams

In April, 2007, the Santa Fe River was designated America's most endangered river by the organization American Rivers. The New Mexico Historic Preservation Alliance followed up by naming the river as one of the twelve most endangered sites in New Mexico. Indeed, from the viewpoint of water flow, it could hardly be considered a river at all. It was completely dry except for a few weeks during a wet spring. However, that didn't mean that on some level the river didn't exist, and exert its influence over the town. When the Watershed Association asked local writers to examine the river, I set off on a field trip close to home.

Its source was in the watershed in the Sangre de Christo mountains, and then reservoirs. I spent a peaceful morning near the reservoirs at the Audubon Center. I wanted to think about the river and what it meant to me.

I was raised on the mighty Hudson River, which divided New York and New Jersey. Cut by a glacier, the river bed at that point actually ran with the tides from the Atlantic Ocean. We were proud of its width and breadth, plied by tugboats and barges, spanned by the exquisite suspension of the George Washington Bridge. Nothing could be more different from the dry river before me.

That description wasn't always true of the Santa Fe River. In fact, its water encouraged the building of nearby pueblos and later Spanish villages. Our plaza and cathedral were situated, if not exactly on, then quite nearby, the river. In fact, the whole center of town was shaped by it. From the Audubon Center, I headed down Cerro Gordo Canyon, cut by the river. The river headed west, into the neighborhood I had lived in for over twenty years. The river park, just a few blocks away, was a place we liked to stroll on cool summer evenings and warm autumn afternoons. We didn't consciously think much about the river bed, but it still helped shape our world. What we did think about, every day, was water, or the lack of it. We conserved it carefully, planting drought-tolerant plants, watering on our assigned days. Our toilet was low flush, and water could be carted by hand from the kitchen sink to the container garden.

And we waited for rain. In summer, if we were lucky, the monsoon rain was our afternoon matinee show. I'd spent countless hours under the front portal, simply watching the clouds and waiting for precipitation to fall. In winter, we tried not to complain about whatever hassles snowfall might create, because "we need it." A native New Mexican friend told me "A real New Mexican, as he sees his house being carried away in a flood, says, 'well, we could use a little more moisture.'" When my daughter was a small child, she shocked her step-grandparents by running out into the rain in Boston. She dashed from the pizzeria, took off her jacket, and stood facing heavenward in an attitude of prayer. Not done in places wetter than ours, she soon discovered, but rain-worship nonetheless.

The major component in the human body is water. Water is our first home inside our mothers' wombs. "Water is life" is not just a slogan. And there was hope for the river. I went down to the village of Agua Fria to look at the work that has been done by the San Ysidro crossing. This was a riparian restoration project. The river doesn't need to flow all year to restore the habitat along it. Rather, flow needs to be controlled so that floods don't erode. Even an ephemeral stream flow can restore the cottonwood bosque along the banks. Youth Works had been picking up trash so the stream bed wasn't a dumping ground. I checked the box on my water bill that would allow a small monthly payment to go towards the city's acquisition of water to aid the river.

Along the Santa Fe River, I was on familiar home territory. In a way, it was the center of my world. But I did not stay home to write about it. In search of the focus brought by solitude and enclosure, I went away for two nights to my private writing spot—a cheap motel at the Albuquerque Airport. This habit of mine has long been derided by my friends and family. They suggest what seem like pleasant alternatives—a hot spring, a housesit, even a nice hotel. But I crave the anonymity, the sense that once that motel door is locked no one and nothing can disturb me. And secretly I like being at the airport, with its sense of departure.

Locked in with a motel desk and some take-out barbecue, I spread out the notes I had on the river. First I laid the poem out by hand in a black notebook, then typed it up. My journey downriver was mapped, but I'd had to leave home to see it clearly.

Water fills my dreams. When I was pregnant and after my daughter was born, I often dreamed of us in the water. The river may be dry, but it does not have to remain that way. It is no coincidence that the church in Agua Fria and the River Park are both named for San Ysidro—patron saint of farmers and agriculture, an icon of rain.

ON THE SANTA FE RIVER

1. Randall Davey Audubon Center

Walled garden set
Among dry red hills.

Fountain, a simple stone
Bubbles over—

Talking water
Out of the living rock,

Hummingbird,
Orange-tipped winged black butterfly,

Yellow butterfly on a field of lavender,
Yarrow.

Like any Impressionist
I sit on the bench in my straw hat:

Creation is born
Of name and water.

2. Cerro Gordo

The child says:
"A river, sometimes
it has water in it,
sometimes it doesn't..."

Not the rivers
I grew up with
But my daughter, born here,
Thinks of river
As dry course.

River did cut this canyon.
Wear down rock
Riddled with ancient shells
Mementos of a sea
Long ebbed away.

The poet Phil Whalen,
Zen priest,
Lived in the little temple here
By Cerro Gordo Park,
Stupa properly situated
Between a turtle-shaped hill
And a river. He used to say:
"One day
we'll just turn on the faucet
and sand will pour out..."

And once, when the kids were little,
My friend Hope and I
Scrambled down the bank
Took them hobo-ing

Along the weedy track
Until we tripped an electronic eye
Heard the canned voice warn:
GET BACK, GET BACK,
THE POLICE WILL BE CALLED.
We hadn't realized this way
Was anyone's private property.

3. Alameda

At the corner of Palace and Alameda
There is a descanso
For JJ Vigil
Who hung, or swung
Into sheer space from the bridge
And died—
Memorialized
By plastic blue hydrangeas,
An American flag,
Bouquets of grief and remembrance.

A little farther upstream, at the corner
To the turn
To Atalaya School
My daughter and I saw each morning
A llama and a donkey,
And we'd sing out—llama!
Pronouncing it correctly
The totem animals
For each day's elementary.

What is the source of my water?
Reservoir, and should it fail
The wells.
Decade of drought
Has coated my tea kettle
With residue of hard water,
Scum of minerals.
What is the source of my water?
Body, rain, memory, dream.

4. Alto Street

spiderweb
on the mailbox
still waiting

half tame sparrows
the house cat
watches

bad news
from everywhere—
what's for supper?

slow stars
above my house
year after year

even the memory
has begun to fade
hazy moon

moonstones
wrapped away—
like a forgotten dream

midnight loud crickets
still no sound
of the key in the lock

rain catches me—
I stayed too long
gossiping

sweeping the dust
under the rug
she writes a poem

5. Justice Department Santa Fe Internment Camp

A Maxfield Parrish sky
Hill overlook
A courting couple sits
He, long-haired and dark, perches
On the granite boulder
That marks the Japanese internment camp.
She, bleached blonde and pierced,
Says: I come here all the time
But I've never read the marker
All the way through.
He looks at the long view of the city
Says—What happened? Did somebody die?
Sunset pinks the Jemez to the west,
Below, we find the red roof
Of St. Anne's, blocks from our house,
Upriver, the campanile
Of the Bataan Memorial Building.

Footprints, bird tracks, anthills
Ephemeral as haiku
Wind writing on sand
There's nothing left but dust,
Those memories.
Somehow, we've been remiss.
In the new suburban neighborhood
Split levels lit with fairy lights at solstice
Or equinox's candled Jack-o-Lanterns.
Land rolls down to the river,
The Feed Lot, the laundromat, pizzeria, and a place for chai.
Along the banks, sculptures
Lift stars or airplanes high
Above the bear claw grasp of time.
Foot bridges cross, no water beneath.
Heavens roll to the abyss.

6. Frenchy's Field

Water doesn't flow through the dry river
Water carves the land, leaves a wadi, an arroyo, a wash
Water can lift up your house and carry it away
On its feet of flash flood
Water composes most of my body
Is colorless, tastes of the end of thirst
Water in glasses, common, critiqued
Ask for it without ice, with lemon, in bottles
As if it weren't already rare and precious
All day we ask ourselves and everyone else--will it rain?
Water consoles me with its tears
Water is in my name
Miriam's Well, a source of water in the desert
That follows us like a shadow, an angel, a mother
With a watering can
This water from an unseen source
No hydrologist can find
Only a prophet
I came from a place with water
And I knew nothing about it
Now I know it takes a shape
From any cupped hand.

7. San Ysidro Crossing

sunflowers, purple peas
two white cabbage moths
sky gone cumulus
stone ledge, lizard
swale

what's dry wash,
passable, or waterfall
what designates the name
trash heap, or river—
saint's prayer,
rain.

IV

Petrified Forrest, Arizona, May 2008:
Time Made Visible

My cabin at the Petrified Forest National Park was both remote and within range of civilization. The cabin had been built by the CCC during the Depression, and it sat on a rise across from what had been a historic hotel and was now a visitors' center on the rim of the Chinle badlands. It was one comfortable room and a kitchen. There was no desk, so I wrote on the kitchen table. At night the spring wind rattled so much that I had to prop a kitchen chair beneath the doorknob to keep the noise down. Coyotes howled, hunting under the moon. The sun rose very early, as Arizona is not on Daylight Saving Time. Some windows faced east, and I'd get up, sketch or write, and sometimes go back to sleep. By the time I woke for breakfast, there might be tour buses with a hundred tourists admiring the spectacular view from the rim I now thought of as mine. In the distance, I-40 rolled west along the Route 66 cut. Cell reception was excellent.

At night I could see the far lights moving between Gallup and Holbrook, with its motel where you could sleep in a fake tepee. Late in the evening a ranger would drive the length of the park and then turn around and drive back. I'd note the headlights. Then the gate was locked, the rangers all in housing just outside the park proper. Unless there were a few hardy souls camping out in the waterless badlands, I was alone in the park. One night I was truly startled out of my skin by a knock on the door. Having read too many Tony Hillerman novels I peered out anxiously, convinced I'd see something terrifying--either human or supernatural. Instead I was greeted by the patroling ranger, who said "Ma'am, just checking to see if you're ok. Didn't see your car move today." I explained I'd just been walking around, and yes, writing. It was nice to be checked up on, but somehow most satisfying to be alone.

I had been here before. The first time was on a trip with my family over the holiday season of 1965-1966. I was almost twelve years old, and what I knew was New Jersey. The exotic and spacious was limited to an annual trip to Cape Cod. But now visions of the west spread out before me. What I glimpsed from the train, from the rim of the Grand Canyon, from a walk through the Petrified Forest was not just a landscape but a sensation. It was something I would long for but not readily identify. When I moved to New Mexico in 1984, by seeming happenstance, that feeling which had lain dormant was reawakened.

And now here I was, surrounded by the rainbow rings of petrified wood. Of course it was illegal, immoral, and all but irresistible to pocket a bit of this petrified wood. Walking along the trail and looking at the gigantic fallen logs of the Triassic now turned to multicolored stone--jasper red, mariposa lily yellow, crystal white—I knew I had to do something before the urge overwhelmed me. I went into the curio store and spent fifty dollars on two beautiful pieces of polished petrified wood collected outside the park. I even bought a small box of polished chips--so smooth, so many colors-- and put them in one of the two bowls in the cabin. This petrified wood existed on a scale of time I could note but not truly imagine— 225 million years ago.

I explored every marked view and geologic wonder of the park, on foot and by car. I liked the fact that I could go "downtown" to the east entrance and order eggs and coffee, buy a necessity or two, and set up my laptop to catch the wireless on a quiet picnic table. The artist-in-residence program's administrator and the resident archeologist took me out for a memorable day where we saw petroglyphs and ruined pueblos built of petrified wood. They took me to "Clambodia"—a large area of clam and worm fossils. Following their example, I started looking at the ground, and could soon find fossil bones of the creatures who had lived here when it was swamp.

I had invited my husband Rich to join me for the last two days of my stay. We then planned to go on to the north rim of the Grand Canyon and Monument Valley. After the quiet of the park it was an adventure to go to Gallup to meet his train, although under usual circumstances I would hardly consider it an exciting city. I was very happy to see him climb down on to the platform, a romantic ren-dezvous with its feel of a bygone era. Then we drove back to the park, and punched in the code. The gate opened and once again I was impressed by the isolated splendor of my cabin.

Then Rich walked in, and put his backpack on the chair. A sim-ple act, but one that made me realize I had company. This chair was not for backpacks, or sitting, it was my "poetry viewing chair" where I arranged drafts. But that wasn't something I could explain to someone else.

Rock Shop

On I-40
Two-headed dinosaurs
Sell beer, ice cream, moccasins
At the rock shop
Slag glass glitters in piles
Swirls of color without
Crystalline structure
The price of prehistoric teeth
On E-Bay drops
When they're reclassified
As crocodilian, not dinosaur
The fans want
Those giant lizards

Tiny glass jars
Hold desert scenes
Painted in sand
Blue mesa, red rock, the view
From the bus
(Could that be us?)
And a cactus
In a painted pot
From somewhere else

Once in the Everglades
I saw a cormorant, smart bird,
Beat a catfish it had caught
Break the invasive species's spine
And swallow it
Not whole but bit by bit
Learned behavior
Hunger that looked like wrath

A tourist took a photograph

VIEWS OF THE PAINTED DESERT

1. The Tepees

Sunrise over the Painted Desert
Dawn's striations illuminate
Colored bands of the Chinle Formation
Lava cap, white sandstone, dark red iron stained siltstone
Red base of hematite
And the dark carboniferous layer of life.

Pangaea broke and floated north
You might name these layers of sediment
Call them:
The trip we took in 1965,
The year he broke my heart,
The day I moved to San Francisco,
The wedding day, the cremation,
That nice time we had
With the kids in the motel swimming pool,
An east coast rainy afternoon.

The present sits on top
I'm here alone
Where earth has pitched her tents
Where wind wears things down
And continental drift
Builds things up.
Rolling in and rolling out
The low sea is gone
For the moment
Or eon.

2. Triassic

Ancient soil horizons, Blue Mesa point
Where fossils calve out of formations
Petrified logs seem birthed
By erosion, wind and rain
Out of Triassic sleep.
What you haul up
Grotesque, but imagined
(You knew the monster there)
Coelacanths, all teeth
That catch, then hold
This dream's heavy weight.
Lungfish too,
That still live today
Can leave water, breath air
Reverse environment
Something we can't do
Would call it drowning
Were sea still here.

Living in the Upper Triassic
By the scenic rim
This layer of life ran
Thousands of miles presumed along a mountain range
To where I was born, New Jersey's Palisades
Large scale rift break-up
Alluvial fan
Newark Supergroup beneath Passaic and Paterson
I never knew was there
Phytosaurs, like crocodiles,
And fossils of raindrops
Ripple marks, pollen

A fossil trace
Of self.

The skeletons were there
In the Museum of Natural History
As for me, I didn't feel real
Till I went west and saw that I could see
Earth's bones.
But still, it was all there
Something beyond
The definition of hunger
Ravenous
Will eat what it must eat
And eat it whole.

3. Puerco Pueblo

At the edge of   Chaco
To the west
Of the center of the world

The Puerco River is dry

Square kiva
    not a cloud in sight
    packed up
    the children
    the narrative of
    footprints in sand

A desert god
Some call horizon

Three thousand stars in this quadrant of sky

Another spiral, an arrow even
Petroglyph etched in the desert varnish
What it takes to survive

Three thousand dancers
On the Pow-Wow floor
Gathering of nations
Eagle held to the four directions
Jingle dress, bead, feather

And how to stay alive
A golden trail
White echo

The wind from here to Mexico

4. Painted Desert Inn
   after Fred Kabotie
   Hopi artist

A panoramic view
Vanishing point
Rustic hotel
Poised on...

Mural of memory
Hosts the sun
Rainbow outline
3 mountain peaks
3 eagles, one on each

We see what we see
Lizard, so quick
See it because we've seen it painted frozen
On the inside of a pot
Or butterfly inlaid semi-precious
At the Best Western Shop

Salt journey
Between the child and the adult
Between home and away and back
Dangers of the four-legged and two-legged sort
And time's three legs

When you return
Nothing is the same
Worlds go up and down
Swallow, rabbit, snake, corn
Day by day, your new name.

5. Curio

In 1965, my father took us on the train
From Chicago, the Super Chief
To the Grand Canyon
I was eleven
Almost twelve, in trouble at school,
Failing French and not
Living up to my potential.

That trip changed everything
For me, I stopped
Suffering, and bought myself
A mud-headed clown kachina
Holding a tiny doll of the same.

I brought home two pieces
Of petrified wood
From the Painted Desert
And later, from New Mexico
A chunk of lava and a penny-sized glass bottle
Full of White Sands.
And made as a science class project
A model of Carlsbad Caverns in a hatbox
Out of melted Hanukah candles
And a pocket mirror.

I loved how the souvenir
Stood for the whole
How years later
I could remember the Alvarado Hotel train station
After it was torn down
I knew I'd been somewhere
Else, out of my own skin.

Tonight, the full moon
Hangs enormous, and then rises
Over the Chinle badlands
The reason I'm here to see it
Is what spoke to me
Just at the edge
Of childhood.

6. Dream

You tried to cure yourself
With beauty
Its pierce, its ache

And partially succeeded
As if to innoculate

This was the mind
Also—not it

A bird's eye view
Of the self
    Acoma
    Casino
    San Francisco Peaks

O water bowl

Recollection

Soon an accumulation of things on the window sill
Comes to represent the desert beyond.
A little altar to color in the smeared pastels:
The box of old rose and yellow green,
Pale orange sunrise. chrome, dusk's Russian blue.
A pile of polished bits of petrified wood
Packaged up for sale, a souvenir
Of what we felt, or felt we saw—
A larger piece, bark mineralized intact
The inner rings of agate, crystal white,
Might make memento or a paperweight,
Collect dust.
Experience can be wrapped for sale
What is time to the entrepreneur
80 million or 200 million years
As long as you can sell
Time's extinction.
A postcard of the petroglyph
Is not the rock, the mark, migration.
I'm not the first, or last, to pass through here
And want something of beauty for my own—
I buy a pair of turquoise and coral earrings—
Dune, earth, and sky—
And thread them through the holes
And wear them home.

Petrified Forest Haiku

the flicker
of the lizard's tail
tells me I'm home

gibbous moon—
two cottontails leaping
over each other

let's just agree
it was a tohwee, that flash
of black and orange

corrugated
potsherd—ripple
of a fossil sea

apricot globemallow
beside the pueblo
of petrified wood

mountain pepperwort
full of fierce wild bees
no thought

the moon set—
two roadrunners,
first white yucca

the fossil fern—
a feeling of what I've tried
to hold on to

4 o'clocks
bloom pink—just
as the dream fades

painting
the desert rain
with gold ink

wondering if
it will rain again
jackrabbit ears

gaming chip
perfectly formed, black and white
pueblo ruin

I'll blame the rain
for the money I spent—
Two Gray Hills rug

my heart pounds
even after decades
meeting your train

Zuni fetish
lizard with turquoise eyes
to remind me

Nizhoni Point

a white butterfly
three black spots inked on each wing
opens
to an iridescent thorax
floats by me
as a I sit
above the salt and crystal
striations of the Chinle badlands

From the Air Quality Monitoring Station

Mound daisies,
Grasslands, as far
As the eye...
Stopped by blue mountains
Called the White Mountains
Vague silhouette
Southeast, clouds that
Imitate, low-shape
In the sky

By the air quality monitoring station
Hum, little rain
Particulate
Of climate shift
Chipped points of Folsom
Beautiful core
Of crystalline petrified wood
Yellow and jasper
Cores either chipped to flake
Or stripped down
To some essential shape.

Migration—
Where did we
Come from?
A thousand years of low-tide
Across the Bering
Or early, slow, down
Coastline no longer there
In boats of skin
Coracle, kayak, a word
In a lost language.

As for me,
I took I-40.
This used to be
The entrance to the park,
In 1962, or '63.
Bisected by sixty trains a day.
The dry wash full
Of invertebrate fossils
Coral worm markings
In the Permian pebbles,
And what you pick up
Is a bit of armored skeleton
Out of the Triassic
In your palm.

At the ruined agate house
Pottery, bold black on white
Bits scattered thick mosaic beneath our feet
A carpet of sherds and petrified wood
And offerings of turquoise
Weathered out
Lying on the caliche underfoot.

Stone mano and metate,
Abandoned, grind only sand.
I'm not the only one
Who, before I must depart,
Wants to pull my house down.

Black Field Sketch

drawing the moon
in white pastel
on black paper

parthenogenic
plateau striped whiptail lizard
replicates herself

a cache of eggs
drawing the moon
in black ink

on black paper
cycad fossil's
monoprint

drawing the moon
in black ink
on white paper

the dream that knocked
white flower skyrocket
pale trumpets

drawing the moon
in white pastel
on white paper

trying to answer
with this—
a flower in an earthquake

V

Stone Quarry Hill Art Park, Cazenovia, New York, June, 2009: The Mythical Upstate

Growing up in northern New Jersey, upstate New York seemed to me to begin immediately just by heading north along the Hudson. I'd never been to true upstate New York, but it had a sound that haunted my imagination, rather like Patagonia or the Arctic. When I applied for a residency at Stone Quarry Hill Art Park I knew I was doing something unusual. The sculpture garden housed only sculptures, and no poet that anyone could ever remember had been in residence there. But being a poet in a sculpture garden had the same archetypical pull as upstate. I wanted in to this terrain of the imagination.

When I arrived I was given a pleasant room, and offered a drill press! It became an ongoing joke between me and the helpful staff that I needed nothing in the way of sculptural equipment or supplies. Getting a table to write on, though, was another matter. I made do with an old beat up card table that I covered with fabric from a local store.

Before I came to the Art Park I spread out a map of New York, the mythical upstate. Looking at it and seeing the place names was like being thrust back in history, particularly to the 19th century when the region, far from being remote, was an epicenter of liberal and radical thought. New York State was a hotbed of progressive and utopian ideas in the 19th century, of everything from abolition to women's rights to the building of the Erie Canal. It even housed Oneida, the community of free lovers whose ideas of group marriage had influenced the 1960's. I began to see the Art Park as a center of a wide circle, a circle that moved back in time, including history and even geology. This was a sculpture garden after all, and I was reminded of Wallace Stevens's poem "I Placed A Jar in Tennessee." Surely even one image, one piece of art, let alone a whole garden, could anchor both past and present around itself. My project was to create a "Poetry Trail Guide" of poems that could be read at specific points in the park, and also the surrounding area.

I had learned from my residencies in the National Parks that I could venture out, notebook in hand, and capture poems as if they were photographs or wildflowers I was identifying. At the Art Park, brilliantly green meadows gave way to forests, to nooks and crannies, ponds and vistas, all full of sculpture, both modern and avant-garde. My first day, on a morning too foggy to drive, I wandered about in pine woods coming upon shapes and images that materialized out of the mist.

My first field trip was to the Oneida Community. After confusing it at first with the town of the same name, I found the enormous mansion that housed what is considered to be 19th century America's most successful experiment in utopian living. Founded by John Humphrey Noyes and active 1848-1880, the residents shared property and a complex marriage.

Then I went off to Seneca Falls, to see where Elizabeth Cady Stanton had proclaimed the "Declaration of Sentiments of the Rights of Women." The Park Service provided a fine museum, and the text of the Declaration carved in stone with a waterfall coursing over it. I burst into tears. My mother had always been a huge fan of Elizabeth Cady Stanton, and now I was standing where she'd stood. My life was actually profoundly different because of the way she'd lived hers. In addition, bits of the Erie Canal were everywhere. In a way, everything else hinged on the canal, which brought ideas as well as goods along its course.

But at the Art Park I was surrounded not just by sculpture, history, and nature, but by working sculptors. They'd disappear mysteriously to the workshop at the top of the hill and come back after dark, tired, dirty, and exhilarated. The landscape kept changing because of them. An exhibition was coming up, and pieces were arranged and rearranged. Just looking out the window could be a source of surprise.

    while I was napping
    the sculptor set torsos
    of forked tree branches

dancing
in the new mown field

This was the work of Deborah Redwood, an Australian artist. Towards the end of my stay, we decided to do a collaboration. She often worked with salvaged and recycled material, and had a roller from a discarded printing press in hand. Of course that was symbolically perfect for a poem. I wrote a haiku-esque text for the roller. And then I began to think like a sculptor. We needed materials—a stamp kit to add the words. We couldn't find one locally. I ordered one from Amazon, worried it wouldn't come in time. It did, but not with the necessary ink pad. Deborah sanded and re-sanded the roller and attached it to a base so it stood like a mini-obelisk. Late at night, we added the letters, using what was at hand—red paint. It read:

lost words
skywriting
fireflies' Morse code

The poems I wrote were collected into a "Poetry Field Guide" to the Art Park, which was given away to visitors. The little sculpture was shown at the gallery at the Park. The ink pads arrived a few days after I departed.

Body Of

lake
body of water

canal
body of work

yellow mustard field
body of evidence

meadowlark
body of liberties

forest
body of knowledge

dream
body of research

fireflies
body of principals

mist
body of water

The Meditation Hut

is falling down
moss grows untended
on the stones
each year, the forest's loam
thickens

burn it
it turns to ash

these thoughts are a pile of sticks
still
it is an unfamiliar bird that whistles
this afternoon

certainly the quality of darkness
is different after midnight
and those twelve chimes
speak of impermanence

bury it
it turns to earth

Chittenango Falls

Back in the Devonian, minus 400 million
When we weren't here

Nor was this continent
That later would house upstate New York

Pangaea floated at the equator
Flooded with warm shallow seas

Went north, all shale and limestone
Sedimentation full of coral, sponge, and mollusk fossils

Met a glacier
In years measured only in thousands

A timeline that might mean something to us
When there were already people and dogs

As there are today in the park
By Chittenango Falls

Where so much water, pure white and powerful
Hurtles and cascades down

A glacial division of the stream
Through the gorge

So green this summer afternoon
Our own small portion of the sublime.

Into the Piney Woods

This was the green beauty of my childhood
A yellow field of mustard
The rain with its rhythm of downpour and lull
The sense of enclosure

In a forest not for Hansel and Gretel
Where real words appear on little signs on the trees
Words that describe the forest
And someone has taped
Small, brilliant, colored tags
Like a riot of Band-Aids
To make a trail
The kind you can see inside a prism
Or double rainbow as the plane
Rises above the clouds

So there is no need for bread crumbs
Because I have an umbrella
I've borrowed from the one I love
Without permission

It is simple here
What is mowed is a meadow
And where roots make sculpture in the shade
Is called woods for the right reason

It is impossible to be lost
Strolling between sleep and waking
A prayer not so much for an angel
But to enter the world.

Tree House

In childhood, where the surface
Was so clean and tidy

I could only suspect
Something underneath.

Even my mother's house
Had its own private life

The creaks and meows of night,
Shadows of the copper beeches.

Out in the woods, there was a clearing
Called Flat Rock

As if this bit of glacier ground granite
Had some kind of intimate meaning to be named,

And Black Bear, which was an enormous
Mass of fungus hanging high in the maples

Like a tumor, or a warning
Or a sign of guardians.

So little was left of the wild
Except for the story

Where Baba Yaga, the witch,
Russian as my grandparents,

Flew through the air
And where her house, the one that walked on chicken legs

Could speak, and always turn towards you
As if we both knew what we wanted.

Untitled #2

I bought a yellow broom
Although I am just visiting

To match the field of mustard
The wind sculpture flags that cross an acre

And the seemingly ownerless
Pair of flip flops at the bottom of the stairs

For how else am I to sweep
Clean and purify the lintel

Show that I am a good woman
Who cares about the floor

How else am I to separate
What I know from what I must learn

And fly through the air all night
And visit you in your dreams?

Oneida

"Looking back upon it
I do not wholly
Understand it, nor
Do I understand and approve
Of all that experience..."

Like figures in an idealized mural
Of garlanded Hope—
The dour formal portraits
Of the free lovers
Lips pursed, pose stiff
Victorian in expression
Who lived in a complex
Group marriage
And manufactured silver spoons
Read Darwin's *On the Origin of Species.*

"A kind of love...
That was a source of torment"
Lock away the sheet music and the violin
To curb the individual's striving,
Free labor and free love,
Leaves and flowers pressed in our Bible.
A cabinet of curiosities
Includes an ostrich egg, a Chinese child's primer,
Shells, rose quartz, chopsticks.

Gold, pink, pale blue—
Our spools of thread,
The requisite needle
A braided tapestry called
"This Is Not Of Man's Devising"

Showing: morning, noon, and night
Then: Birth, Love, and Death.
An album quilt,
Each patch from a different woman
United into the whole—
Croquet, a musical note,
Bees in a hive, children at play with a wooden horse,
Ark beneath a rainbow,
A bunch of grapes,
A dove of peace.

"I should not like
To go to heaven
And find it like Oneida."
Still, so powerful an idea
You might find yourself
More than a hundred years later
In a communal house
On the Mission or the Haight
Grappling with the same notions
Saying of our shared life:
This is a table,
Eat at it.

Secret Garden Trail

Why must inspiration be a vista?
Remembered peonies are beaten down by rain
Into their impressionistic essence.
A formal garden in the mind's eye
Blurs in all this mist
And the dark alley between trees
Is scattered with pine cones, cinquefoil, trillium.
In a sculpture garden
Even the mushrooms
Seem placed on purpose.
Once, half-lost, I turned in a cul-de-sac
And saw through a gap
A pond full of water lilies
In all directions—
An inner self
That also shifts shape.

Seneca Falls

Knitting Factory reflected in the dark canal,
Water cascades down the wall of carved words,
Filling every letter with reflection,
Declaration of Sentiments of the Women's Rights Convention.

Water cascades down the wall of carved words
"At first we traveled quite alone..."
Declaration of Sentiments of the Women's Rights Convention
"Long before we reached Seneca Falls we were a procession"

At first we traveled quite alone.
The landscape is green and marked by orange lilies.
Long before we reached Seneca Falls we were a procession
That reached into a limitless future.

The landscape green and marked by orange lilies.
"He has endeavored in every way...to destroy her confidence in her
own powers"
That reach into a limitless future—
"To lessen her self-respect...make her...dependent and abject..."

He has endeavored in every way...to destroy her confidence in her
own powers.
"How I do long to be with you this very minute"
To lessen her self-respect...make her...dependent and abject
"To have one look into your very soul"

How I do long to be with you this very minute.
"I am in the sunset of life."
To have one look into your very soul
"My special mission is to tell people what they are not prepared to hear."

I am in the sunset of life.
Knitting Factory reflected in the dark canal.
My special mission is to tell people what they are not prepared to hear—
Filling every letter with reflection.

Stone Quarry Hill

In the late afternoon thunder
Green fields turn greener
And lightning strikes
A little too close.
I go downstairs and heat water
For tea on glowing coils.
If this poem were Chinese
I'd say my hair is gray (which it is)
And that I haven't heard
News of you for a long time.

Erie Canal

Compresses time and distance
Shows belief
In the perfectibility of (man)kind.
For us, Providence created the gap in the mountains
Where once continents collided, then drifted
Apart.

A housewife on the barge, curtains, geranium, a cat,
Children reading.
Does Nature = God?
The canal, which, man-made
Becomes as uncontrollable as the sea
Without a Sabbath.

Past Chittenango, New York
Where Frank Baum was born
And what better utopia than Oz?
Where today there is a yellow brick road sidewalk
And a sign: Got Life Insurance?
"Wicked Witch Never Saw It Coming!"

Neoclassical temple in the park.
In the book, the enchanted boy
Becomes Ozma, the glittering princess
Oddly satisfying to my childhood mind
Like the army of girls with knitting needles.

Ideas of liberation towed along
The path with mules and barges
"Failure Is Impossible."

Dark water is shallow
Weedy with fish shadow
And a song.
Locks defy sea level
And white blossoms float along in early summer.

VI

Mounds, August 2007-April, 2009:
In-Between Places

I'd always wanted to see the mounds, those great earthworks left behind by the native civilizations of what is now the American southeast and midwest. Some are platform pyramids, some conical, many are mortuary, and some served an unknown purpose.

And a great many have been lost—flattened by the plow, bulldozed by developers. Some have been preserved in anomalous settings, like golf courses. I was fascinated by the archeology of the Adena, Hopewell, and Mississippi cultures. Also, the mounds are truly an intersection between the suburban and a much more ancient world.

My exploration of this zone began with a major life change in my family—my daughter went off to college in Ohio. We dropped her off with all the attendant emotions and then visited the mounds of Cahokia, which was once a huge city. It stands today in Illinois, across the river from St. Louis.

The next trip to Ohio was also in the service of a ritual transition—my nephew's bar-mitvah. My husband Rich and I went to various sites before and after—Fort Ancient, the necropolis group at Mound City, which is part of the Hopewell National Historical Park, Seip with its grassy green mounds, and even Serpent Mound. This last, in Peebles, Ohio, is the largest effigy mound of its type in North America. We went on to search for some mounds in Cincinnati and to Angel Mound in Indiana.

One more family occasion led me back. I celebrated my fifty-fifth birthday with my sister's family and my daughter. And saw Newark earthworks, a huge octagonal site once linked to others by the Hopewell road.

The major sites were impressive and and intriguing, but the

small mounds that cropped up in odd places were equally interesting. They sat in and next to libraries, sports fields, cemeteries—marking the landscape of exurbia. Although really it was that landscape that obtruded on them.

Of all the places in this project, this was the most dispersed in time and space. The visits were spread over almost two years, and what I was looking for was a remnant rather than a specific place. In a way, the mounds were located more in the past than in the present, and they were a link to a mythic underworld, to something archetypical. The poem I wrote about Serpent Mound was also part of a larger project, a collaboration between writers and visual artists at Gallery 516 in Albuquerque. We were given themes, but not each other's work. When I got up to read my poem I found myself in front of a gigantic image of a snake.

The process of writing the poems wasn't unified. I wrote in motels along the way, and in my study at home. Towards the end of the project I found I had more to say, and sat writing on the couch, hemmed in by piles of art books on artifacts from the mounds.

Throughout it all, these was a kind of poetic tourism. In suburban Cincinnati, at the Oddfellows Cemetery, we cruised with a mounds guidebook in hand. Here were 19th century graves marked by classical columns, urns, and obelisks—these last monuments Egyptian and therefore somehow suited to the dead as if these middle-class Germans were pharaohs. Names erode from the softer marble but not the granite.

the tops
of abandoned grain silos
festooned in trees

Flag limp in the breezeless day. And a mound—covered in grass and trees—in the center of the graveyard. This was a burial mound too, probably of the Adena people. Once these mounds were everywhere by rivers and flood plains. There was also another mound here, small and spotted with the incursion of graves.

And there was a large mound in Water Tower Park, which itself was just a strip of green alley between family houses. The mound was somber, looming, overgrown. Artifacts might include bones, a shaman's pipe, bronze antlers, hands carved in mica.

a dark feeling
in the maze
of dreams

Plastic swing sets littered the lawns, and the water tower also
loomed. This was an in-between place. Facing the street was a white
Victorian, gray shingled, with a handsome wraparound porch.
There were so many levels of time here that memory could not un-
ravel them.

house on a small hill
beneath a running sky
storm clouds, then thunder

Mound

Red ocher on burial bones.
A mound in Pickerington, Ohio,
Between houses on a suburban street.
Sign reads:
    "Prehistoric—Adena culture—
    No sledding."

Enon Mound. By the library
In the middle of Indian Mound Estates.
    stone altar.
    who hasn't felt
    the rat's bite loss of grief
    and wanted to slaughter.

Cahokia. Green mound 72.
20,000 marine shell beads
shaped into a platform
in the image of a raptor
53, 24, 22, 19—mass burials
    girls + women
    15-25 years
451 arrow points
(heads cut off
replaced
    by pots)

what the shaman sees from the air
serpent mound or
St. Louis, Missouri
    tall grass prairie
persimmon, paw paw
lotus, pokeweed, bloodroot

this figurine—possibly of a woman
is either
transforming corn into flour
or causing rain

black soil
of sacrifice
tracked on my sneakers
to this bed

underworld
    sleep
    dream
conical mounds, platforms
snake   gourd vine

to return over and over
to an image
as if it were real

Midden

Shell middens haunted my childhood
Where were they—those great piles?

Left behind, by people older than my grandparents
And long gone

On the beaches of what will be Manhattan
Or in the Everglades mangrove swamp of standing trees

How people who never saw mountains
Built them, platforms for the gods

And there are others too
Beneath the earth

With the bones arranged
Tidied for re-birth

Motif of the bird of prey
The mortuary mounds

That in this light seem so benign
Seem to swell away

In a sea of grass
Where you can picnic

On Memorial or Father's Day
And not have to ask

What is underneath

Serpent Mound

Coils in green grassy embankment
Holds in its mouth
   an egg
   a world
   us
Maps on the earth
Celestial comet, or constellation
Draco, moonrise, solstice
Equinoctial heartbeat
Switchback
Where light rises, throbs, stands still
Like a knife to the heart of sacrifice.

Effigy figure of a woman hoeing a snake,
The museum label reads "a legend"
Might be
   metaphor
   narrative
   the truth

thistles, clover, Queen Anne's lace
cicadas seventeen years underground
the dreaming nymphs emerge
bug-eyed and winged
and butterflies:
mourning cloak, sulphurs,
confusing cloudywing, pearl crescent, blues—
so many butterflies
you want to close your eyes
and dream of transformation

sacrifice of turquoise
blue veins of earth's pulse
lying open to the sky

ask for rain
peace
in a prayer
that petitions without vowels

vessel, urn, skull

the ferocity
of pots

pot shaped like a black dog
as if to avoid
or remember
sacrifice

cauldron, incense burner
guarded by
the serpent mask
body's cranium and pelvis
contain our nature's
cannibal stew--
good, and its opposite,

child's cradle
baby's basket set afloat
until the infant is pulled out--
Quetzalcoatl feather--
pulled out of the river

Newark Earthworks

octagon   intersects
golf course

the mound versus the plow

tiny wild violets and white cup flowers
underworld, which is now
the soil of Ohio

curved obsidian knife
used only for sacrifice
    harsh glint

Wendy's, McDonald's, Waffle House

ceremonial road
    without wheel

conjoined mounds
where today
people run their dogs
in the grassy quadrant

and the morning star
is off playing hardball
beneath the earth

Newark High School Athletic Complex
mound littered with cans
sacrifice of virgins
maybe on prom night
easy to scramble up

underwater panther
who rules a realm
of dreams beneath the rippled surface
effigy pipe
    smoke hole   yurt
housepole
shamans out of pan-Siberia

Hunter

slingshot carved
in the shape of a woman
bent backward

hit bird
falls out of the sky
like a stone

meteor blazes
into atmosphere
feathered plume

goddess dancing hoops on the horizon

Untitled 3

after all these years
you came to me in a dream
you said you were well
your head was shaved
you had a woman
and enough money

the corpse pipe
found in a mound
is the body of a corpse
(tobacco in the head)
even the inexpensive
reproduction
is so frightening
I keep it wrapped

Indian pipes
pale luminous fungus
spring up after rain
beneath the pines

a needle can also thread
a bone can also
play the wind

VII

Andrews Experimental Forest, October, 2009: Compost

I was a little bit nervous about my arrival at Andrews Experimental Forest in the lower Cascades. I didn't know what to expect, and in my mind's eye the forest had become more remote and even intimidating each time I thought about it. It had been a long time since I'd lived among trees. The final instructions I'd gotten from the staff about my weekend arrival were—we'll just leave the house open for you. I had an image of being Goldilocks, including the bears.

But I drove from Eugene through some lovely country (river gorge, apple orchards) and arrived in the midst of gorgeous old growth forest (ferns, moss, salamanders, huge trees). And immediately was greeted by the sociable sight of a mushroom class strolling out of the woods with hands full of psychedelically yellow chanterelles. And instead of the rustic cabin I was imagining, I had an apartment—really too big for one person but fine. There was a phone right in the office.

In my imagination this old growth forest in the Cascades had been unconnected to my life in New Mexico or even to much of anything around it. It was a green island floating in time and space. There was no cell phone reception so I'd imagined a lonely pay phone lit by a yellow light bulb. But Andrews was more peopled than I'd realized and it was a research station after all.

At Andrews, I felt the intersection of humankind and the wild. There were very tame deer and fawns who were no longer being fed but who had good memories and weren't shy of humans. There was a little pond of koi who surfaced at the sound of human feet, expecting food.

I settled into my apartment. On the linoleum of the kitchen was the giant image of a mushroom. These fungi would soon become my totem in Andrews, for they were everywhere.

The next morning I had a wonderful time getting oriented by an ecologist and former writer-in-residence named Tim. He had spent a decade studying spotted owls. He took me to two of the three designated "reflection points"—these are the spots set aside for observation for 200 years, and each writer who stays in the forest writes about them. First, a clearcut with replanted trees which was so horrifying in the context of this forest. Although I'd seen such cuts before I had underreacted. This was like seeing people or animals being mistreated—and I understood the trees as living beings, not as resources.

Then we drove to a remote-seeming old growth/log rot area—I got a good explanation of the ecosystem as a whole and could distinguish the canopy. I soaked it up in case I didn't have the nerve to traipse that far in alone. However, I soon found myself in possession of a field radio and began to feel more secure in the woods.

The third plot was a gravel bar right near the apartment—its theme was flood as the site had been created by the force of water. It was literally in my backyard, and I visited it many times. The first time I went out I was dashing, trying to see it before the rain got more intense. I forgot my walking stick, slid down a bit of incline, and wondered how I'd get back up. Looking around and pausing for a moment, I realized I was surrounded by potential walking sticks. A gnarled broken branch, dripping moss, graciously allowed itself to be used.

There was also an experimental flume where researchers sent down soil and mud to understand landslides, a pretty dramatic mechanism in the landscape. Here, the earth itself was volatile with mud slides so slow the naked eye could not see them, and with volcanic activity. My friend Pat drove all the way from Corvallis to visit. We'd met when we were sixteen, and marveled that we still had a lot to talk about. She brought me a quiche made with chanterelles, and drove me into the lava fields above the Andrews, and all the way to Sisters. The mountains were obscured by clouds. The next day it snowed and the pass was closed for the season.

I felt I'd gone native when I soaked in a local hot springs in the rain—something a New Mexican would never do. But it was pointed out to me that if Oregonians didn't soak in the rain they would almost never get to soak at all. In the forest, I went to sleep very early, sometimes waking at dawn to write in bed. I loved just taking the compost out. I'd see a new kind of mushroom or fungus every day by the pile. The forest itself was of course a vast compost. And so it seemed was my imagination.

Mushroom Pantoum

beyond the peaks
beneath the earth
in the dark of sleep
intricate, enormous mushroom network

beneath the earth
nitrogen in soil, fixates
intricate, enormous network
fungi, mites, nematodes, protozoa

nitrogen in soil, fixates
mushroom larger than leviathan
fungi, mites, nematodes, protozoa
white rust, black spot, blue mold, canker rot

mushroom larger than leviathan
or anything that walks on earth
white rust, black spot, blue mold, canker rot
the rustling of beetle galleries

anything that walks on earth
was it supposed to grow that big?
a rustling of beetle galleries
mushroom = fungal fruiting

was it supposed to grow that big?
this self from before the kalpas—eons
mushroom = fungal fruiting
clouded salamander, clouded mountain

this self from before the kalpas—eons
beyond the peaks
clouded salamander, clouded mountain
in the dark of sleep

An Autobiography in Trees

Afraid in my mother's house at night in the wind
Stand of hemlocks three times as big as the house
Pointed starward—and rustled—
A world up to no good.
Shadow, headlight, streetlamp, the ceiling alive
With pattern,
And a child in bed.

Or waking, hearing how in the storm
A tree crashed into the neighbor's roof
And came within inches
Of crushing the children
A story the hired help told
With more interest than sympathy.
Or how at my grandparents' lawn party
When the huge tulip tree, rotten at the heart
Split, and my little sister
Started running and reached the canopy
By the time the tree hit earth
Bruised but all right.

How as a young woman I lived on the point of the beach
Each night the trees
Seemed to come closer to the house
And I'd turn on the floodlights
To wait.

How the god Pan is panic,
Fear of being lost in the woods
How here in the old growth in middle age
I saw the big leaf mßaple fall and
Fall, red mushrooms poke
From earth, a salamander
Slide away
And dreamed all night
Of another part of the forest.

Rustic

Entering this world's
Ink washed scroll
Up the MacKenzie River
Past apple orchards,
Mist starting to burn off,
Yellow leaves fall
Visible in slow motion
Palmate leaves as big
As a baby's head
Or both my hands.

This yellow
In the Chinese black
Landscape
Of Oregon
Makes me think of Phil Whalen
Or a Gary Snyder poem
And although I was expecting
The solitude of rain on my arrival
Emerged into sunshine.

If old growth means never logged
Then I am not old growth—
Fern, moss, lichen, nurse log—
I've ben cut, and more than once,
Who hasn't, by middle age.
But there's a salamander glistening in the shade
Red and brown, a silky soil
And the yellow leaves that fall apart
Like water in a gorge
Could cover my fisted heart.

Reflection Points

> *"Only a while ago all mountains moved in fire."*
> —Yosano Akiko

Clear cut—rows of dollar signs instead of Douglas Fir
Lower Lookout on 1501
hill of colored scrub and madrone
trucks that carry out not just logs but nutrients
farm not forest.

Lookout Creek at 1506
great logs allowed to fall by time, time's gravity
first seedling shoot towards an opening in the canopy
the cycle's obvious
could be viewed as romance
of interdepedence
how a stump becomes a hassock of brilliant moss
or viewed as waste—no profit here—
just mosaic, spectrum.

yew draped in moss
the forest holds a cure
for what ails, or will ail us,
standing snags—
trees that refuse to fall
scorpions in the depths of forest floor,
mushrooms glistening like mother-of-pearl.

pink flags mark the strands of false broom
like a tiny installation by Christo,
a plastic wrap
of an invasive species
still—barred owls fly out of their range
to spotted ones
might compete, or mate—

it's not as if we knew what we were doing either.

water's force took the curved road out
it sounded metallic, like a huge gamelan
playing as rock tumbled forth
from the slow slide gone mad.
the gravel bar
beside the stream,
red alders fixing nitrogen
and how you get here?
simply enter the gap
in the trees
and proceed through green.

earth moves so slowly you can't see it move
takes years to tumble down the hillside
yet move it does
the physics of the flume, strong as desire

reflection means to think but also
to see by means of visible light
in the old growth—
this world, this self.

A Different Forest

The woman at the hot springs
Asks what brings me here
I say I'm staying in the forest
But she mishears
And thinks I've come to visit
A local boy named Forrest
Who lies unconscious in the hospital
After a terrible car wreck.

I don't want to be reminded
Of the descansos on Old Las Vegas Highway
Four crosses in pastels and purples
For the kids killed that night
By a drunk driver
Or the sound my daughter's friend made
When she heard,
A sound beyond weeping.

Logging trucks go by in the mist
Like a line of oversized hearses
All around me
The forest is awake
With its moss-draped yew trees
Its beetles and fungi stirring a tree trubk
To ferny soup.
Only I am sleeping.

Two Tanka

your small clay teacups
with pinch pot impish faces
seem to contain
river, falls, mist, rain
a whole watershed of dreams

compost bin buried
in yellow big leaf maple
mushrooms shine gray, red
in the rain, and I believe
they are dreaming of me

Forest Haiku

waxing moon
in the mist—
fir, cedar, hemlock

STOP sign
in the old growth forest
covered in moss

torrential rain—
doe and fawn have come close
to my house

dream of coffee cake
and loss
but not of you

in the moss forest
tiny mushrooms
loom enormous

raindrops
in the hotspring—
concentric circles

rainbow
over the lava fields—
stark white tree trunks

just as I left
I saw the geese
also flying south

something shining
on a moonless night
led me home

Aubade

making love to you
in the single bed
in the forest
I drop an earring
black and silver beads
I bought from a Navajo woman
on the rim of Canyon de Chelly

that was a thousand miles from these firs and hemlocks
and a long time ago, too
but even then I was with you
though after a long absence

walking along the forest floor
you tell me how your time at the Pacific
reminded you of the desert
the same feeling—
maybe it was the horizon line
or the availability
of vastness

mushrooms—orange fairy caps and honey—
release their spores,
why, standing upright
is the future in front of us
the past behind?

my dreams have gills
can leap, amphibious,
although I'm never going back
to the place where I was born
but place
the unfamiliar cup
on the unfamiliar table
and move on.

What Am I?

feeds on decay, is phosphorescent

scavanger that cannot move

sometimes poison, sometimes food

on the forest floor a perfect ring

umbrellaed with a cap and stem

destruction turned to luminescence

Untitled #4

can't place the melody
   at 3 a.m.
tiny orange ears
   of mushrooms
      poking through fallen needles
open to cups
   that catch rain
   a snatch of
      Mozart?
      DNA?
   in the trembling wood.

Spore Print

gills laid to white paper
on an overcast day
sketched in mushroom ink

coral fungi
no shell
no sea

the way we floated on the lake
above the trees petrified in lava
how it gave the children nightmares

how what we ignored or couldn't explain
remained in plain view
while looking down

until one day
the surface of the water
simply filled with clouds, with rain

Nocturne

loneliness whistles
with the tea kettle

and it is hard
not to feed the fawn
the doe with the cougar-bitten ear

snow
on the far ridge of mountain

raven is here, as expected
impossible to live
in a world without crows

when I was young
I suffered, wondering if you loved me

now ask the same of god.

Notes

In "Saint in a Landscape" the quote "earth's surface and the figments of the mind have a way of disintegrating" is from Robert Smithson.

The title "From Air to Air" came from a phrase of Pablo Neruda's.

The quotations in the poem "Oneida" are all from women who lived there.

In the poem "Seneca Falls"; the first quote is from Charlotte Woodward, 1848. The second is modified from an article in the "Declaration of Sentiments." written by Elizabeth Cady Stanton. The third is a letter from Susan B. Anthony to Stanton. The fourth quote is from Elizabeth Cady Stanton.

About the Author

Miriam Sagan has published 25 books, including *Map of the Lost*. She founded and directs the creative writing program at Santa Fe Community College, and has won a Border Library Association Award, a New Mexico Book Award, Best Memoir from Independent Publishers, and the 2011 Santa Fe Mayor's Award for Excellence in the Arts.

Colophon

This book was created using using Quark XPress.

The text and display type are set in Veljovic,
designed by Jovica Veljovic, a type designer, typographer and pro-
fessor of design and typography born in 1954 in Yugoslavia.